Foreword

The world of work is changing rapidly, and remote work is at the forefront of this transformation. As more and more people turn to remote work as a means of employment, it's important to have a guide to help navigate the challenges that come with this new way of working.

"Thriving in the Digital Age: A Remote Worker's Survival Guide" is an essential resource for anyone who is looking to succeed as a remote worker. From dealing with the isolation of working from home to managing your time effectively, this book covers everything you need to know to thrive in the digital age.

As a remote worker myself, I can attest to the challenges that come with this lifestyle. It can be difficult to stay motivated and productive when you're working from home, and it's all too easy to fall into bad habits. But with the right mindset and the right tools, remote work can be incredibly fulfilling and rewarding.

This book is a valuable resource for anyone who is looking to make the most of their remote work experience. It's packed with practical tips, expert advice, and real-world examples that will help you succeed as a remote worker.

Contents

Introduction 2

Part I: Setting Yourself Up for Success 3

Chapter 1: Making the Transition to Remote Work 5

Chapter 2: Setting Up A Remote Workspace 21

Chapter 3: Managing Your Digital Environment 31

Part II: Staying Productive and Focused 39

Chapter 4: Staying Motivated and Avoiding Distractions 40

Chapter 5: Managing Your Time Effectively 43

Chapter 6: Staying Healthy and Active 45

Part III: Navigating the Challenges of Remote Work 47

Chapter 7: Dealing with Isolation and Loneliness 48

Chapter 8: Building and Maintaining Relationships 51

Chapter 9: Managing Your Workload and Boundaries 53

Part IV: Advancing Your Remote Career 55

Chapter 10: Building Your Personal Brand 56

Chapter 11: Networking and Finding Opportunities 57

Chapter 12: Thriving in the Remote Workforce 60

Conclusion Appendix: Resources for Remote Workers
Acknowledgments 62

Introduction

The world of work is changing rapidly, and remote work is at the forefront of this transformation. As more and more companies adopt remote work policies, and more people choose to work from home, it's clear that this is a trend that is here to stay. And while there are many benefits to working remotely, such as greater flexibility and autonomy, it's not without its challenges.

As a remote worker myself, I know firsthand the unique set of challenges that come with this way of working. From dealing with the isolation of working from home to managing your workload and boundaries, it can be a daunting experience, especially if you're new to the world of remote work.

That's where this book comes in. "Thriving in the Digital Age: A Remote Worker's Survival Guide" is a comprehensive guide to help you navigate the challenges and opportunities of remote work. Whether you're just starting out or you're a seasoned remote worker, this book has something for you.

In this book, you'll learn how to set yourself up for success, stay productive and focused, navigate the challenges of remote work, and advance your remote career. You'll discover practical tips, expert advice, and real-world examples that will help you thrive as a remote worker.

I wrote this book because I believe that remote work has the power to transform the way we work and live. But to make the most of this opportunity, we need to be equipped with the right knowledge and tools. I hope this book will serve as a valuable resource for you, helping you unlock your full potential as a remote worker and achieve success in the digital age.

Part I: Setting Yourself Up for Success

The key to thriving as a remote worker is to set yourself up for success from the very beginning. In this section, we'll cover the essential steps you need to take to ensure that you have the right tools and environment to be successful in your remote work journey.

Chapter 1: Making the Transition to Remote Work

In the first chapter, we'll explore the transition to remote work and what you can expect in terms of changes to your work routine and lifestyle. We'll provide practical advice on how to stay productive and focused in your new environment, and how to adjust to the unique challenges that come with remote work.

Chapter 2: Setting Up Your Home Office

Your home office is the heart of your remote work environment. In chapter 2, we'll show you how to set up a comfortable and ergonomic workspace that will help you stay focused and productive. From choosing the right desk and chair to setting up the right lighting and temperature, we'll cover everything you need to know to create a workspace that works for you.

Chapter 3: Managing Your Digital Environment

In the digital age, your online presence and environment can have a huge impact on your success as a remote worker. In chapter 3, we'll explore the tools and technologies that can help you stay organized, connected, and productive. From project management tools to communication platforms, we'll show you how to build a digital environment that supports your remote work goals.

By the end of Part I, you'll have the foundational knowledge and resources you need to set yourself up for success as a remote worker. Whether you're just starting out or you're looking to improve your existing setup, the strategies and insights in this section will help you thrive in the digital age.

Chapter 1: Making the Transition to Remote Work

Making the transition to remote work can be a significant adjustment, especially if you're used to working in a traditional office environment. In this chapter, we'll explore the changes that come with remote work and provide practical advice on how to stay productive and focused in your new environment.

Understand the Benefits and Challenges of Remote Work

Before making the switch to remote work, it's essential to understand both the benefits and challenges that come with this way of working. Remote work offers greater flexibility and autonomy, but it can also be isolating and require more self-discipline. Understanding both sides of the coin will help you set realistic expectations and be better prepared for the transition.

Benefits of Remote Work:

1. Greater Flexibility: Remote work offers the flexibility to work from anywhere, at any time.
2. Increased Autonomy: Remote workers have more control over their work schedule and environment.
3. Improved Work-Life Balance: Remote work can allow for more time with family and friends, and the ability to pursue personal interests.
4. Reduced Commuting: Remote workers avoid long commutes, which can save time and reduce stress.
5. Lower Costs: Remote work can reduce expenses associated with commuting, eating out, and office attire.
6. Increased Productivity: Without the distractions of a traditional office environment, remote workers can often be more productive.
7. Access to a Global Talent Pool: Remote work allows businesses to hire talent from around the world, increasing diversity and expanding their talent pool.
8. Better Health: Without the stress of commuting and exposure to illnesses in the office, remote workers often have better mental and physical health.
9. Reduced Carbon Footprint: Remote work can reduce carbon emissions associated with commuting and office energy usage.

10. Increased Job Satisfaction: Remote workers often report higher levels of job satisfaction due to the flexibility and autonomy remote work provides.

Challenges of Remote Work:

1. Isolation: Remote work can be isolating, leading to loneliness and decreased social interaction.
2. Lack of Structure: Without the structure of a traditional office environment, remote workers must create their own routine and discipline.
3. Communication Challenges: Communication with team members can be challenging, leading to miscommunication and misunderstandings.
4. Difficulty Collaborating: Remote workers may face challenges collaborating with colleagues due to physical distance and lack of face-to-face interaction.
5. Time Management: Without the structure of a traditional office environment, remote workers must be disciplined in managing their time and avoiding distractions.
6. Technology Issues: Technical issues can arise, such as poor internet connectivity or computer malfunctions, causing delays and interruptions.
7. Blurred Boundaries: Remote work can blur the lines between work and personal life, leading to burnout and decreased productivity.
8. Lack of Personal Interaction: Remote workers may miss the personal interaction and social aspects of a traditional office environment.

9. Increased Responsibility: Remote workers may face increased responsibility for their work and must take ownership of their tasks.
10. Difficulties in Disconnecting: Without a clear separation between work and personal life, remote workers may struggle to disconnect from work and may experience work-related stress even during off hours.

Overall, remote work offers many benefits but also presents several challenges that must be managed effectively to achieve success as a remote worker.

Establish a Routine

One of the most significant changes when transitioning to remote work is the lack of structure that comes with working from home. Without the regular routine of commuting and being in an office, it can be challenging to establish a consistent work routine. Creating a schedule and sticking to it can help you stay focused and productive.

Here are ten ways to establish a routine when working remotely:

1. Set Regular Working Hours: Establish set working hours and stick to them as much as possible. This will help create a clear structure

to your day and make it easier to manage your time.

2. Create a Dedicated Workspace: Designate a specific area of your home as your workspace. This will help you create a boundary between your work and personal life and make it easier to switch off at the end of the day.
3. Take Breaks: Taking regular breaks can help you stay focused and productive. Use this time to stretch, take a walk, or engage in other activities that help you clear your mind and recharge.
4. Plan Your Day: Before starting work each day, create a to-do list outlining your tasks for the day. This will help you prioritize your work and ensure you stay on track.
5. Use Time Blocking: Time blocking involves allocating specific periods of time to different tasks throughout the day. This can help you stay focused and make the most of your time.
6. Establish a Morning Routine: Create a morning routine to help you start the day on the right foot. This could involve exercise, meditation, or simply taking time to enjoy a cup of coffee before starting work.
7. Avoid Distractions: Distractions can quickly derail your workday. Turn off notifications on your phone, and resist the urge to check your email or social media during working hours.
8. Set Boundaries with Others: Let others in your household know your working hours, and ask

them to respect your designated workspace and work schedule.

9. Create an End of Day Routine: Establish a routine to signal the end of your workday, such as shutting down your computer, taking a walk, or engaging in a non-work activity. This will help you transition out of work mode and into your personal time.

10. Evaluate and Adjust: Regularly evaluate your routine and adjust it as necessary to ensure it continues to work for you. This can involve adjusting your working hours, changing up your routine, or experimenting with different productivity strategies.

By following these tips, you can establish a routine that works for you and helps you stay focused and productive while working remotely. Remember, finding the right routine may take some trial and error, but with time and practice, you can develop a routine that helps you thrive in your remote work environment.

Set Boundaries

When you work from home, it can be challenging to separate your work and personal life. Establishing clear boundaries and sticking to them is essential to maintaining a healthy work-life balance. This can include setting specific work hours, creating a dedicated workspace, and limiting distractions.

here are five ways you can set boundaries when working remotely:

1. Create a Dedicated Workspace: Designate a specific area of your home as your workspace, and use it exclusively for work-related tasks. This will help create a physical boundary between your work and personal life.
2. Establish Clear Working Hours: Set specific working hours and communicate them with your team and anyone you live with. This will help establish clear boundaries around when you are available to work and when you are not.
3. Turn Off Work Notifications: When you're not working, turn off notifications related to work emails, messages, and calls. This will help you disconnect from work and prevent work-related interruptions during your personal time.
4. Learn to Say No: It's important to know your limits and say no when you need to. This could include saying no to taking on extra work or setting limits on when you're available to take meetings or calls.
5. Establish Communication Guidelines: Set expectations for how you prefer to communicate with colleagues, such as which channels to use for urgent matters and how often you check in. This can help prevent work-

related stress and interruptions during your personal time.

By setting boundaries in these ways, you can create a healthier work-life balance and maintain your mental and emotional wellbeing while working remotely. Remember, it's important to communicate your boundaries clearly with your colleagues and those around you, and to stick to them as much as possible to avoid burnout and maintain a healthy lifestyle.

Stay Connected

Working remotely can be isolating, so it's important to stay connected with your colleagues and the outside world. Regular communication with your team, whether it's through video calls, instant messaging, or email, is essential to maintain collaboration and productivity. It's also essential to make time for social interactions outside of work to maintain a healthy work-life balance.

here are ten ways to stay connected when working remotely:

1. Use Video Conferencing: Video conferencing is an excellent way to stay connected with colleagues and clients, allowing you to have

face-to-face conversations even when you can't meet in person.

2. Use Instant Messaging: Instant messaging tools like Slack or Microsoft Teams can help you stay connected with your team throughout the day, allowing you to quickly ask questions, share updates, and collaborate on projects.

3. Schedule Regular Check-Ins: Schedule regular check-ins with your colleagues or team members to stay connected and ensure everyone is on the same page.

4. Participate in Virtual Team Building: Participate in virtual team-building activities, such as online games or virtual happy hours, to build camaraderie and maintain a sense of team spirit.

5. Use Collaboration Tools: Use collaboration tools like Google Drive or Dropbox to share and work on documents together, even when you're not in the same physical space.

6. Attend Virtual Conferences: Attend virtual conferences or webinars to stay up-to-date on industry trends and connect with others in your field.

7. Join Professional Organizations: Join professional organizations or associations related to your industry to stay connected with others in your field.

8. Use Social Media: Use social media to stay connected with colleagues and clients, share

updates about your work, and engage in conversations with others in your industry.

9. Participate in Online Forums: Participate in online forums or discussion groups related to your industry to ask questions, share ideas, and connect with others.

10. Reach Out Personally: Reach out to colleagues or clients personally through phone calls or email to stay connected on a more personal level.

By using these methods, you can stay connected with colleagues and clients, build relationships, and maintain a sense of community even when working remotely. Remember, staying connected takes effort and intentionality, but the benefits of maintaining these connections are well worth it.

Manage Distractions

When you work from home, there can be many distractions that you wouldn't encounter in a traditional office environment. From household chores to social media, it's essential to manage these distractions to maintain focus and productivity. Strategies can include setting aside specific times for breaks, using time management techniques such as the Pomodoro Technique, and avoiding multitasking.

Distractions can be a major challenge when working from home. Here are twenty ways to manage distractions and stay focused:

1. Set up a dedicated workspace.
2. Establish a routine.
3. Minimize distractions by wearing noise-cancelling headphones.
4. Use time-blocking to schedule your workday.
5. Take regular breaks to recharge.
6. Turn off notifications on your phone and computer.
7. Use website blockers to limit time spent on distracting websites.
8. Communicate with family members or roommates about your work schedule.
9. Keep your workspace clean and organized.
10. Use apps or tools to track your time and productivity.

11. Close your office door or put up a "do not disturb" sign.
12. Take advantage of natural lighting to improve focus.
13. Use a white noise machine to block out distracting noises.
14. Use a standing desk or balance ball chair to stay active while working.
15. Use background noise or ambient music to help you stay focused.
16. Take advantage of the Pomodoro technique by working in focused bursts.
17. Use a separate phone line or email for work.
18. Prioritize your tasks and tackle the most important ones first.
19. Use a task management app to stay organized.
20. Practice mindfulness or meditation to help manage stress and stay focused.

By implementing some or all of these strategies, you can manage distractions and stay focused while working from home, ultimately improving your productivity and job performance.

Invest in the Right Equipment and Technology

Investing in the right equipment and technology is essential for remote work success. This can include a reliable internet connection, a comfortable chair and desk, and a reliable computer. It's also important to have the right tools to communicate and collaborate with your team, such as video conferencing software and project management tools.

By following these practical tips and strategies, you can make a smooth transition to remote work and set yourself up for success. With the right mindset, routine, and tools, you can thrive in your new work environment and enjoy the many benefits of remote work.

Here are ten pieces of equipment and technology you may want to consider investing in:

1. Laptop or Desktop Computer: A reliable computer is essential for remote work. Consider investing in a high-quality laptop or desktop computer that meets your specific work requirements.
2. External Monitor: An external monitor can expand your workspace and help you stay productive. Consider investing in a high-resolution monitor that is compatible with your computer.
3. High-Speed Internet: A fast and reliable internet connection is crucial for remote work. Invest in a high-speed internet connection that meets your work requirements.
4. Noise-Cancelling Headphones: A good pair of noise-cancelling headphones can help you stay

focused and block out distractions when working from home.

5. Webcam: A high-quality webcam is essential for virtual meetings and video conferences. Consider investing in a webcam that offers high-resolution video and clear audio.
6. Microphone: A high-quality microphone can help ensure that you are heard clearly during virtual meetings and conferences.
7. Wireless Keyboard and Mouse: A wireless keyboard and mouse can help you work comfortably and efficiently, without being tethered to your computer.
8. Printer: Even in a digital age, a printer can still be a valuable tool for remote workers. Consider investing in a high-quality printer that meets your specific needs.
9. Project Management Software: Project management software like Asana, Trello, or Basecamp can help you stay organized, collaborate with your team, and track project progress.
10. Cloud Storage: Cloud storage services like Dropbox or Google Drive can provide secure storage for your work files, allowing you to access them from anywhere and collaborate with others easily.

By investing in these pieces of equipment and technology, you can set yourself up for success when working remotely and stay productive and efficient while working from home.

Chapter 2: Setting Up A Remote Workspace

One of the most significant benefits of remote work is the ability to work from anywhere, including the comfort of your own home. However, in order to be productive and successful as a remote worker, it's essential to have a dedicated and functional office.

In this chapter, we'll explore the key elements of setting up a remote office that is conducive to productivity and focus. We'll cover topics such as selecting the right location, creating a comfortable and ergonomic workspace, and selecting the essential equipment and technology needed for your job.

We'll also discuss best practices for organizing your workspace, such as decluttering and implementing effective storage solutions. Additionally, we'll explore how to create a pleasant and stimulating environment that can help boost your creativity and productivity.

By following the advice and guidance in this chapter, you'll be able to create a home office that allows you to work comfortably, efficiently, and effectively. You'll also be able to optimize your workspace to meet the unique demands of your job and work style, ultimately helping you achieve success and fulfillment as a remote worker.

Selecting The Right Location

When it comes to setting up a home office as a remote worker, selecting the right location is crucial. Your home office location should be conducive to productivity, focus, and comfort.

Here are some tips for selecting the right location for your home office:

1. Consider your work style: Think about your work habits and style, and choose a location that aligns with your needs. For example, if you prefer a quiet and private space, consider setting up your home office in a spare bedroom or unused corner of the house.
2. Assess the lighting: Lighting is an important factor when selecting a location for your home office. Choose a location with ample natural light or invest in proper lighting fixtures to reduce eye strain and improve productivity.
3. Check for noise: Avoid locations with high traffic areas or other sources of noise that can distract you from your work. If you can't avoid noise, consider investing in noise-cancelling headphones or a white noise machine.
4. Ensure privacy: If your work involves confidential information, select a location that provides privacy and security. This could be a room with a door that can be locked or a separate building on your property.
5. Evaluate accessibility: Choose a location that is easily accessible, especially if you have clients or colleagues visiting. Consider setting up your home

office near the front entrance of your home or in a separate building with a dedicated entrance.

By selecting the right location for your home office, you can create a space that allows you to work comfortably, efficiently, and effectively. Additionally, having a dedicated home office space can help you establish boundaries between work and personal life, leading to a healthier work-life balance.

Creating A Comfortable and Ergonomic Workspace

Creating a comfortable and ergonomic workspace is essential for remote workers who spend a significant amount of time sitting in front of a computer. Poor ergonomics can lead to discomfort, fatigue, and even injury over time. Here are some tips for creating a comfortable and ergonomic workspace:

1. Choose a comfortable chair: Invest in a comfortable, adjustable chair that provides adequate lumbar support and can be adjusted to your height and weight.
2. Position your monitor correctly: Your computer monitor should be positioned at eye level, with the top of the screen at or slightly below eye level. This reduces neck and eye strain.
3. Use a separate keyboard and mouse: Consider using a separate keyboard and mouse, which can be positioned at a comfortable distance

and angle from your body, reducing strain on your wrists and hands.

4. Adjust your desk height: Your desk should be at the correct height to allow your feet to rest flat on the floor and your elbows to form a 90-degree angle when typing.

5. Use proper lighting: Proper lighting is important for reducing eye strain and headaches. Use a combination of natural and artificial light, and avoid glare on your computer screen.

6. Take breaks and move around: Regular breaks are essential for avoiding fatigue and reducing the risk of repetitive strain injuries. Take frequent breaks and stretch, walk, or do light exercise.

By creating a comfortable and ergonomic workspace, you can improve your physical comfort and reduce the risk of developing injuries or chronic pain. Additionally, a comfortable workspace can increase your productivity, creativity, and overall well-being as a remote worker.

Selecting Essential Equipment and Technology

As a remote worker, having the right equipment and technology is crucial for your success. In this chapter, we'll discuss the essential equipment and technology you need to get your work done efficiently and effectively.

1. Computer: Your computer is the most critical piece of equipment you'll need as a remote worker. It's essential to choose a reliable, high-performance computer that can handle the demands of your work.
2. Internet Connection: A reliable and fast internet connection is critical for remote work. Consider investing in a high-speed internet plan to ensure you can access your work materials and communicate with your team efficiently.
3. Headset: A high-quality headset can make it easier to communicate with colleagues or clients on conference calls or video chats. Choose a comfortable headset with good sound quality and noise-canceling features to block out background noise.
4. Printer and Scanner: Depending on your work requirements, you may need to print or scan documents. A good quality printer and scanner can make this process much more efficient.
5. External Hard Drive: An external hard drive is an excellent tool for backing up important files and documents. Consider investing in a high-capacity drive that is compatible with your computer.
6. Collaboration Software: Collaboration software, such as Zoom, Skype, or Slack, is essential for remote workers to stay connected with colleagues. Choose software that is user-friendly and reliable.

7. Project Management Software: If you work on projects with a team, project management software can help you stay organized and on track. Choose software that fits your team's needs and can be accessed from anywhere.

8. Cloud Storage: Cloud storage solutions, such as Dropbox or Google Drive, are essential for remote workers to store and share files securely. Choose a cloud storage solution that is easy to use and provides the necessary security features.

9. Security Software: Remote workers should invest in security software to protect their devices from cyber-attacks. Choose a reliable and reputable antivirus program to keep your computer and data safe.

10. Ergonomic Equipment: Finally, don't forget about ergonomic equipment. As we discussed in Chapter 2, creating a comfortable and ergonomic workspace is critical for your health and well-being. Invest in a good quality ergonomic chair, keyboard, and mouse to reduce the risk of injury or strain.

By selecting the right equipment and technology, you can set yourself up for success as a remote worker. Take the time to research and invest in the tools that will make your work more efficient and effective, and you'll be well on your way to success in your remote work journey.

Decluttering and Effective Storage Solutions

As a remote worker, your home office is your sanctuary. It's important to keep it clean, organized, and free of clutter to maintain focus and productivity. Here are some best practices for decluttering and implementing effective storage solutions in your home office.

1. Declutter your space: The first step in organizing your workspace is to declutter. Get rid of anything that you don't use or need. This could include old papers, files, and office supplies that are taking up valuable space. Create a designated area for items that need to be discarded or recycled.

2. Maximize storage space: Once you've decluttered, it's time to maximize your storage space. Consider investing in shelves, cabinets, or other storage solutions that can help you organize your office supplies and paperwork. Use labels to keep things organized and easy to find.

3. Go vertical: Make the most of your space by going vertical. Invest in wall shelves or organizers to store items off the ground and free up desk space. This will also help you stay organized and prevent clutter from piling up.

4. Use desk organizers: Desk organizers, such as trays and file holders, can be incredibly helpful in keeping your workspace tidy. Use them to

store important documents and supplies, keeping them within reach but out of the way.

5. Implement a filing system: A good filing system can help you keep your paperwork organized and easy to find. Create folders for different categories, such as client information or project files, and make sure to label them clearly.

6. Minimize distractions: Clutter and disorganization can be a significant distraction for remote workers. Implementing effective storage solutions can help you minimize distractions and stay focused on your work.

By decluttering and implementing effective storage solutions in your home office, you can create a workspace that is clean, organized, and conducive to productivity. Take the time to evaluate your space and invest in the right storage solutions to make the most of your home office.

How to Boost Creativity and Productivity

As a remote worker, your home office is more than just a place to work – it's your personal space where you spend a significant amount of time each day. Creating a pleasant and stimulating environment can help you stay motivated and inspired, leading to increased productivity and creativity. Here are some tips for designing a workspace that will help you achieve your best work:

1. Choose the right colors: The colors you choose for your workspace can have a significant impact on your mood and productivity. Consider using colors that evoke a sense of calm or motivation, such as blues, greens, or yellows. Avoid using colors that are too bright or distracting, as they can make it difficult to focus.
2. Add plants: Adding some greenery to your workspace can help create a more pleasant and relaxing environment. Plants not only add visual interest to your space, but they also help purify the air and promote a sense of calm.
3. Personalize your space: Your workspace should reflect your personality and interests. Add personal touches, such as photographs or artwork, that inspire you and make you feel happy.
4. Use natural light: Natural light is essential for creating a pleasant and stimulating environment. Position your workspace near a window or use light-filtering shades to let in natural light. This will help boost your mood and energy levels, leading to increased productivity.
5. Invest in quality furniture: Investing in a comfortable and ergonomic desk and chair is essential for maintaining good posture and reducing the risk of back pain. Make sure your workspace is comfortable and supportive so

you can work for extended periods without experiencing discomfort.

6. Keep your workspace clean and tidy: A cluttered workspace can be a significant distraction, so it's important to keep your area clean and tidy. Regularly clean your workspace and remove any clutter or unnecessary items that may be taking up valuable space.

By designing a workspace that is both pleasant and stimulating, you can increase your productivity and creativity, leading to more successful and fulfilling remote work experiences. Take the time to evaluate your workspace and make any necessary changes to create an environment that supports your work and inspires your creativity.

Chapter 3: Managing Your Digital Environment

In the digital age, technology plays a crucial role in the lives of remote workers. However, with so many digital distractions and tools at our fingertips, it can be easy to become overwhelmed and lose focus on our work.

In this chapter, we'll explore strategies and techniques for managing your digital environment, including how to effectively use email, instant messaging, and collaboration tools. We'll also discuss how to manage your online presence, maintain digital security, and back up important data.

Additionally, we'll provide tips on how to manage your digital workspace and stay organized using digital tools such as calendars, to-do lists, and project management software. We'll also explore how to integrate mindfulness and meditation practices into your digital routine to help reduce stress and stay focused.

By effectively managing your digital environment, you'll be able to minimize distractions and optimize your productivity as a remote worker. You'll also be able to take advantage of the many digital tools and resources available to you, ultimately helping you succeed and thrive in the digital age.

Managing Your Digital Environment: Strategies and Techniques for Remote Workers

As a remote worker, you rely heavily on digital tools to communicate and collaborate with your team. Managing your digital environment is critical to your productivity and success, and it can be challenging to navigate the various communication channels and collaboration tools available. Here are some strategies and techniques for effectively managing your digital environment:

1. Manage your email effectively: Email can be a significant source of distraction, so it's essential to establish a system for managing your inbox. Consider setting aside specific times during the day to check your email and avoid checking it constantly. Use filters and labels to organize your inbox and prioritize your messages based on their importance.
2. Use instant messaging judiciously: Instant messaging can be an effective way to communicate with your team, but it can also be a significant source of distraction. Use instant messaging tools judiciously, and only for urgent matters that require immediate attention.
3. Choose the right collaboration tools: There are many collaboration tools available, such as project management software, document sharing platforms, and video conferencing

tools. Choose the tools that are best suited for your needs, and avoid using too many tools at once, as this can lead to confusion and inefficiency.

4. Establish communication guidelines: Establish clear communication guidelines with your team, such as response times for emails and instant messages. This will help to avoid misunderstandings and ensure that everyone is on the same page.

5. Limit social media use: Social media can be a significant source of distraction, so it's essential to limit your use of these platforms during work hours. Consider using a website blocker or setting specific times to check your social media accounts.

By effectively managing your digital environment, you can improve your productivity and focus, leading to more successful and fulfilling remote work experiences. Take the time to evaluate your current digital habits and make any necessary changes to optimize your digital environment for success.

Managing Your Online Presence and Digital Security: Best Practices for Remote Workers

As a remote worker, you rely on digital tools to communicate with your team, access important files, and stay connected with clients and customers. However, with increased reliance on digital technologies comes the need for enhanced security and privacy measures. Here are some best practices for managing your online presence and digital security:

1. Create strong and unique passwords: Use a unique and strong password for each of your online accounts. Avoid using common words, phrases, or personal information that can be easily guessed.
2. Enable two-factor authentication: Two-factor authentication provides an additional layer of security by requiring a second form of identification, such as a text message or biometric verification.
3. Secure your devices: Make sure that all of your devices are password-protected, and enable remote tracking and wiping capabilities in case of theft or loss.
4. Back up your data: Back up important files and documents regularly, either to the cloud or an external hard drive, to ensure that you can recover your data in the event of a system failure or data breach.
5. Be mindful of your online presence: Be mindful of the information you share online, both in terms of personal information and opinions. Avoid oversharing personal information and consider using a VPN to encrypt your online activity.

6. Use reputable software and services: Use reputable software and services that are known for their security and privacy features. Be wary of unknown or untested apps or software.

By implementing these best practices, you can protect your personal and professional data, maintain a secure online presence, and reduce the risk of data breaches or cyber attacks. Remember to stay vigilant and up-to-date on the latest security and privacy measures to ensure that you are always protected.

Managing Your Digital Workspace: Tips for Staying Organized and Productive

As a remote worker, your digital workspace is just as important as your physical workspace. With so many digital tools available, it can be overwhelming to keep track of everything. Here are some tips for managing your digital workspace and staying organized:

1. Use a digital calendar: Use a digital calendar, such as Google Calendar or Outlook, to keep track of important dates and deadlines. You can also use the calendar to schedule reminders and block out time for focused work.
2. Create to-do lists: Use a to-do list app, such as Trello or Todoist, to keep track of your daily tasks and projects. Organize your to-do lists by priority or deadline, and break down larger projects into smaller, manageable tasks.

3. Use project management software: If you work on collaborative projects, consider using project management software, such as Asana or Monday.com, to track progress, assign tasks, and communicate with team members.
4. Organize your files: Use a cloud-based storage system, such as Dropbox or Google Drive, to store and organize your files. Use descriptive file names and folder structures to make it easier to find what you need.
5. Use keyboard shortcuts: Keyboard shortcuts can save you time and help you navigate your digital workspace more efficiently. Take the time to learn the most common shortcuts for your operating system and software.
6. Minimize distractions: Use software, such as RescueTime or Focus@Will, to block distracting websites and apps. You can also use a noise-cancelling headset or background noise app to minimize auditory distractions.

By implementing these tips and utilizing digital tools, you can streamline your workflow, stay organized, and be more productive in your remote work environment. Remember to regularly evaluate your digital workspace and make adjustments as needed to ensure that you are using the most effective tools and strategies.

Integrate Mindfulness And Meditation Practices

In today's digital age, it can be difficult to disconnect from technology and find moments of peace and calm. Remote workers often face even greater challenges in finding balance between work and personal life. Mindfulness and meditation practices can be powerful tools for managing stress, improving focus, and increasing productivity.

In this section, we'll explore how to integrate mindfulness and meditation practices into your digital routine. We'll provide an overview of the benefits of mindfulness and meditation, including improved mental clarity, reduced stress and anxiety, and better emotional regulation.

We'll discuss different types of meditation, including guided meditations, breathing exercises, and body scans, and provide tips on how to find the right practice for you. We'll also discuss how to create a meditation practice that fits into your busy work schedule, whether it's a brief morning meditation or a longer session during lunchtime.

In addition, we'll explore the benefits of incorporating mindfulness into your digital routine. We'll discuss techniques for staying present and focused during work, such as taking regular breaks, setting intentions for the day, and avoiding multitasking. We'll also discuss how to practice mindfulness in other aspects of your life, such as during meals or daily activities.

By incorporating mindfulness and meditation practices into your digital routine, you can reduce stress and anxiety, improve your focus and productivity, and find more balance in your remote work lifestyle.

Part II: Staying Productive and Focused

In the world of remote work, staying productive and focused is essential for success. With the freedom and flexibility that comes with working from home, it can be easy to get sidetracked and lose focus on your work. This can lead to decreased productivity, missed deadlines, and lower job satisfaction.

In this section, we'll explore various strategies and techniques that can help you stay productive and focused while working remotely. From developing a structured routine to managing distractions and taking breaks, we'll provide practical advice on how to optimize your workday and maintain a high level of productivity. We'll also discuss the importance of staying organized, prioritizing tasks, and managing your time effectively.

Whether you're new to remote work or a seasoned pro, the strategies and tips in this section can help you maximize your productivity and reach your full potential as a remote worker.

Chapter 4: Staying Motivated and Avoiding Distractions

Working remotely comes with its own set of unique challenges, including distractions, time management, and staying motivated. In this chapter, we'll explore various strategies and techniques that can help you stay productive and achieve your goals as a remote worker.

1. Set goals and prioritize tasks One of the most important steps to staying productive is setting clear goals and prioritizing tasks. By identifying what you need to accomplish each day, you can stay focused and avoid getting sidetracked by distractions. Use a to-do list or productivity tool to keep track of your tasks and schedule them in order of priority.

2. Establish a routine Establishing a routine is another effective way to stay productive. By creating a daily schedule and sticking to it, you can build healthy habits and improve your focus. This routine should include dedicated work time, breaks, exercise, and time for personal activities. A consistent routine helps to ensure that you are allocating enough time for work and leisure.

3. Use the right tools and technology The right tools and technology can make a significant difference in your productivity. Find tools that

suit your needs and make your work more efficient, whether it's time tracking software, project management tools, or collaboration platforms. Invest in quality equipment, such as a fast and reliable computer, a comfortable chair, and noise-cancelling headphones to create a more conducive workspace.

4. Minimize distractions Distractions can be a significant challenge for remote workers. To minimize distractions, find a quiet and distraction-free workspace, turn off notifications on your phone and computer, and consider using apps that block distracting websites or apps during work time.

5. Take breaks Taking breaks is essential for staying productive. Studies show that taking breaks can help reduce stress, improve focus, and increase creativity. Take regular breaks throughout the day, such as a quick walk or stretching, to improve your productivity.

6. Set boundaries Setting boundaries is essential for maintaining a healthy work-life balance. Establishing clear boundaries between work and personal time can help you avoid overworking and burnout. Consider setting limits on your work hours, avoiding work-related tasks outside of work hours, and learning to say no to additional work requests when you are already busy.

7. Stay organized Staying organized is critical to productivity. Keep your workspace clutter-free,

prioritize tasks based on deadlines, and ensure that you have the necessary resources and tools to complete your work.

8. Practice time management Effective time management is a vital skill for remote workers. Use time tracking tools to monitor your productivity, set clear deadlines for projects, and avoid procrastination. Break down larger projects into smaller, more manageable tasks and schedule regular progress updates to ensure that you are on track.

9. Collaborate and communicate effectively Communication and collaboration are critical components of remote work. Use communication tools such as video conferencing, instant messaging, or email to keep in touch with your team, share ideas and updates, and collaborate effectively.

10. Take care of your physical and mental health Finally, taking care of your physical and mental health is essential for staying productive. Prioritize exercise, eat well, get enough sleep, and practice mindfulness and relaxation techniques to help reduce stress and improve focus.

By implementing these strategies and techniques, you can stay productive and achieve success as a remote worker.

Chapter 5: Managing Your Time Effectively

Managing your time effectively is crucial for remote workers who are responsible for their own schedules. In this chapter, we'll explore various techniques and tools to help you make the most of your time and stay productive.

1. Create a schedule: One of the most important things you can do to manage your time effectively is to create a schedule. This includes setting clear start and end times for your workday, scheduling breaks, and planning out tasks and projects in advance. Use a digital or paper calendar to help you stay organized.
2. Prioritize tasks: Not all tasks are created equal. Use the Eisenhower Matrix or other prioritization methods to determine which tasks are most important and which can wait until later. This will help you stay focused on what matters most and avoid getting bogged down in busywork.
3. Minimize distractions: Distractions can eat up valuable time and disrupt your workflow. Consider using web blocking software to block distracting websites during work hours. Also, try placing your phone on vibrate or turning off notifications during focused work sessions.
4. Take breaks: It may seem counterintuitive, but taking regular breaks can actually help you stay productive in the long run. Use a timer to

remind yourself to take a break every hour or two, and use that time to step away from your desk and recharge.

5. Use the Pomodoro Technique: The Pomodoro Technique involves working in focused bursts of 25 minutes, followed by short breaks. This can help you stay focused and avoid burnout.

6. Set goals: Setting specific, measurable goals can help you stay motivated and track your progress. Use SMART (specific, measurable, achievable, relevant, time-bound) goal-setting to make sure your goals are realistic and achievable.

7. Practice time blocking: Time blocking involves scheduling specific blocks of time for different tasks or projects. This can help you stay focused on one task at a time and avoid multitasking, which can actually decrease productivity.

8. Delegate tasks: If you have team members or colleagues who can help with certain tasks, don't be afraid to delegate. This can help you free up time and focus on higher-priority tasks.

9. Use productivity apps: There are many productivity apps available that can help you stay organized, track your time, and manage your tasks. Experiment with different apps to find the ones that work best for you.

10. Take care of yourself: Finally, don't forget to take care of yourself. Getting enough sleep, exercise, and healthy food can help you stay

energized and focused throughout the day. And remember to take breaks and step away from work when you need to recharge.

Chapter 6: Staying Healthy and Active

When working remotely, it's easy to fall into a sedentary lifestyle and neglect your physical and mental health. However, taking care of yourself is crucial to maintaining your productivity and happiness in the long run. In this chapter, we'll explore various strategies and techniques to help you stay healthy and active while working from home.

1. Establish a regular exercise routine: Set aside time every day for physical activity, whether it's going for a walk, doing yoga, or hitting the gym. Regular exercise can help boost your energy levels, improve your mood, and reduce stress.
2. Take breaks and stretch regularly: Sitting at a desk for hours on end can lead to back pain, neck pain, and other health problems. Taking frequent breaks to stretch and move around can help alleviate these issues and keep you feeling fresh and focused.
3. Practice good ergonomics: Make sure your workspace is set up in a way that promotes good posture and reduces strain on your body. Invest in a comfortable chair, adjust your monitor to the right height, and use a

keyboard and mouse that are comfortable to use.

4. Eat a healthy diet: Eating a balanced diet that's rich in fruits, vegetables, and whole grains can help improve your overall health and energy levels. Avoid relying on junk food or snacking throughout the day, and take time to prepare healthy meals and snacks.

5. Stay hydrated: Drinking plenty of water throughout the day can help you stay alert and focused. Keep a water bottle nearby and aim to drink at least eight glasses of water per day.

6. Take care of your mental health: Working remotely can be isolating and stressful, so it's important to take care of your mental health as well. Practice mindfulness, meditation, or other relaxation techniques to help manage stress and anxiety.

7. Connect with others: Don't let remote work prevent you from socializing and connecting with others. Take time to talk with colleagues, friends, and family members, and consider joining online communities or networking groups.

8. Get enough sleep: Adequate sleep is essential to your overall health and well-being. Make sure to get at least seven to eight hours of sleep each night, and avoid staying up late or working in bed.

9. Avoid distractions: Distractions can derail your productivity and cause unnecessary stress.

Consider using web blocking software, silencing your phone, and placing it on vibrate to minimize interruptions and stay focused.

10. Take time off: Just because you work from home doesn't mean you should be working all the time. Take breaks, schedule time off, and make sure to give yourself time to rest and recharge.

Part III: Navigating the Challenges of Remote Work

As exciting and liberating as remote work can be, it comes with its fair share of challenges. While the flexibility and autonomy that come with remote work can be beneficial, it can also lead to burnout, isolation, and other issues. In this section, we'll explore some of the most common challenges remote workers face and provide practical advice on how to overcome them. From managing distractions to dealing with loneliness, we'll provide you with the tools and techniques you need to thrive in a remote work environment. Whether you're new to remote work or have been doing it for years, this section will help you navigate the challenges and maintain a healthy work-life balance.

Chapter 7: Dealing with Isolation and Loneliness

One of the biggest challenges of remote work is the feeling of isolation and loneliness that can come with working from home. Without the daily interactions with coworkers, it can be easy to feel disconnected and lonely. However, there are many ways to combat these feelings and stay connected with others, even when working remotely. In this section, we'll explore some of the most effective strategies for dealing with isolation and loneliness in a remote work environment.

20 Ways to Deal with Isolation and Loneliness:

1. Join a virtual community of remote workers to connect with others who are in the same situation.
2. Schedule regular video calls with friends and family to maintain social connections outside of work.
3. Participate in online forums or groups related to your industry or interests to connect with like-minded individuals.
4. Consider finding a remote work buddy or accountability partner to help you stay motivated and connected.
5. Take breaks throughout the day to go for a walk, get some fresh air, and interact with people in your community.

6. Attend local networking events or conferences to meet other professionals in your industry.
7. Join a virtual book club or other group focused on a shared interest.
8. Consider coworking at a local space or coffee shop to be around other people while you work.
9. Take an online class or course to learn something new and connect with others who share your interests.
10. Practice mindfulness meditation or yoga to reduce stress and improve overall well-being.
11. Volunteer in your community to meet new people and make a positive impact.
12. Join a sports team or exercise group to stay active and connect with others.
13. Attend virtual social events hosted by your company or other organizations.
14. Use web-based collaboration tools to stay connected with colleagues and collaborate on projects.
15. Take advantage of social media to connect with others in your industry or community.
16. Schedule virtual coffee breaks or lunch meetings with coworkers or other professionals.
17. Set up virtual happy hours or game nights with friends or colleagues.
18. Consider getting a pet to provide companionship and reduce feelings of loneliness.

19. Join online forums or support groups for remote workers to share experiences and advice.
20. Practice self-care by prioritizing rest, exercise, and hobbies outside of work to maintain a healthy work-life balance.

Chapter 8: Building and Maintaining Relationships

Introduction:

Remote work can be a solitary experience, and it's easy to feel disconnected from colleagues and friends when you're working from home. Building and maintaining relationships, both personal and professional, is crucial for your well-being and success as a remote worker. In this chapter, we'll explore practical ways to stay connected with others, build new relationships, and nurture existing ones.

10 Ways to Building and Maintaining Relationships:

1. Schedule regular virtual check-ins with colleagues and friends. Whether it's a weekly video call or a quick chat over instant messaging, staying in touch can help combat feelings of loneliness and isolation.
2. Join online communities and forums related to your interests or industry. This is a great way to connect with like-minded individuals and expand your network.
3. Attend virtual events and conferences. Many events and conferences have gone virtual, offering opportunities to learn, network, and connect with others in your field.
4. Participate in online classes or workshops. Learning something new can be a great way to

meet new people and connect with others who share your interests.

5. Volunteer or get involved in community activities. Giving back to your community can be a rewarding way to meet new people and build meaningful connections.

6. Use social media to stay connected with friends, family, and colleagues. Platforms like LinkedIn, Twitter, and Facebook can be powerful tools for building and maintaining relationships.

7. Practice active listening. When you're communicating with others, make a conscious effort to listen attentively and show empathy and understanding.

8. Offer help and support to others. Being there for others when they need it can help strengthen your relationships and build trust.

9. Be authentic and genuine in your interactions with others. Don't be afraid to show your personality and be yourself.

10. Take the initiative to reach out and connect with others. Don't wait for others to initiate contact - take the first step and reach out to someone you'd like to connect with.

Chapter 9: Managing Your Workload and Boundaries

One of the biggest challenges of remote work is managing your workload and boundaries. When you work from home, it can be difficult to separate your personal and professional life. This can lead to working longer hours, feeling overwhelmed, and burnout. However, with the right strategies in place, you can manage your workload effectively and maintain healthy boundaries.

Managing Your Workload and Boundaries:

1. Set realistic goals: It's important to set realistic goals for yourself and your work. This will help you manage your workload and avoid burnout. Break down large projects into smaller tasks and prioritize them based on their importance and urgency.
2. Create a schedule: Creating a schedule can help you stay on track and manage your workload effectively. Block out specific times for work, breaks, and personal time. Stick to your schedule as much as possible to maintain healthy boundaries.
3. Use web-blocking software: Web-blocking software can help you stay focused and avoid distractions during work hours. These tools can block websites and apps that may be tempting

to visit during work hours, helping you stay on task and improve productivity.

4. Place your phone on vibrate: When you receive notifications on your phone, it can be tempting to check them immediately. Placing your phone on vibrate can help you avoid distractions and maintain your focus during work hours.

5. Take breaks: Taking breaks throughout the day can help you manage your workload and maintain healthy boundaries. Step away from your workspace, stretch, and do something enjoyable during your break time.

6. Learn to say "no": It's important to set boundaries and learn to say "no" when necessary. If you're feeling overwhelmed or overworked, it's okay to decline additional work or ask for additional support.

7. Prioritize self-care: Self-care is important for managing your workload and maintaining healthy boundaries. Take care of your physical, emotional, and mental health by exercising regularly, getting enough sleep, and practicing mindfulness or meditation.

8. Delegate tasks: If you're feeling overwhelmed with your workload, consider delegating tasks to others on your team. This can help you manage your workload and prevent burnout.

9. Use a task management system: A task management system can help you keep track of your workload and prioritize tasks. There are

many tools available, such as Trello or Asana, that can help you stay organized and focused.

10. Establish clear communication: Establishing clear communication with your colleagues and clients can help you manage your workload effectively. Be clear about your availability, deadlines, and expectations to prevent misunderstandings and improve collaboration.

Part IV: Advancing Your Remote Career

As remote work continues to grow in popularity, many individuals are looking for ways to advance their careers while working from home. While remote work can offer many benefits, such as increased flexibility and a better work-life balance, it can also present unique challenges when it comes to career advancement. However, with the right strategies and mindset, it is possible to thrive in a remote career and take your professional development to the next level.

In this section, we will explore various strategies and techniques to help you advance your remote career. We will cover topics such as networking, personal branding, and professional development, as well as tips for staying motivated and focused on your goals. Whether you are just starting out in your remote career or looking to take it to the next level, this section will provide you with the tools and insights you need to succeed.

Chapter 10: Building Your Personal Brand

Building a personal brand is essential in today's competitive job market, and it is no different for remote workers. When working remotely, it can be challenging to make a name for yourself and stand out among the crowd. However, by developing and nurturing your personal brand, you can establish yourself as a valuable asset to your organization and increase your chances of career advancement.

In this section, we will explore the importance of building a personal brand as a remote worker and provide practical tips on how to create a strong and memorable online presence. We'll discuss the elements of a successful personal brand, including your online persona, networking strategies, and the role of social media in promoting your brand. By the end of this chapter, you will have a clear understanding of how to develop and promote your personal brand as a remote worker.

Chapter 11: Networking and Finding Opportunities

In today's digital age, building a personal brand is crucial for professional success. As a remote worker, it is even more essential to develop and promote your personal brand to stand out from the competition and showcase your unique skills and expertise.

Your personal brand is how you present yourself to the world, and it encompasses your values, skills, and personality. It is how you differentiate yourself from others and establish your credibility in your field. A strong personal brand can help you attract new clients, secure new projects, and advance your career.

In this section, we will discuss how you can develop and promote your personal brand as a remote worker. We'll provide you with practical steps that you can take to create a strong personal brand that resonates with your target audience and showcases your unique value proposition. Let's dive in!

1. Define your unique selling proposition: Identify what sets you apart from other remote workers in your field. What are your strengths, skills, and experiences that make you unique? This will help you create a personal brand that stands out.
2. Build a professional online presence: Create a strong online presence on professional networking sites like LinkedIn, remote work

job boards, and your personal website. Make sure your profiles are up-to-date and represent your personal brand.

3. Network and collaborate: Attend virtual networking events, connect with other remote workers, and collaborate on projects. Building relationships with others in your field can help you grow your personal brand and open up new opportunities.

4. Publish content: Share your knowledge and expertise by publishing articles, blog posts, or videos on your personal website or social media. This can help establish you as a thought leader in your field and attract potential clients or employers.

5. Be consistent: Consistency is key to building a strong personal brand. Make sure your messaging, tone, and content are consistent across all your online profiles and communications.

6. Seek out feedback: Ask for feedback from colleagues, clients, and others in your field to help you improve and refine your personal brand.

7. Be authentic: Your personal brand should reflect who you are and what you stand for. Don't try to be someone you're not, as this can come across as inauthentic.

8. Share your successes: Celebrate your successes and share them with others. This

can help you build credibility and establish yourself as a successful remote worker in your field.

9. Emphasize your remote work experience: Highlight your remote work experience and the unique skills and strengths you've developed as a remote worker. This can help differentiate you from others in your field who may not have experience working remotely.

10. Stay up-to-date: Stay informed about the latest trends and developments in your field, and continue to develop your skills and expertise. This can help you stay relevant and grow your personal brand over time.

Chapter 12: Thriving in the Remote Workforce

As remote work becomes increasingly common, it's more important than ever to not only adapt to the remote work lifestyle but to thrive in it. Thriving in the remote workforce means not only meeting expectations but exceeding them and standing out from the crowd. It means being a valuable asset to your company, maintaining a healthy work-life balance, and continuously growing both professionally and personally.

Steps to Thriving in the Remote Workforce:

1. Set clear goals: It's important to set clear goals for yourself both professionally and personally. This will help you stay focused and motivated.
2. Develop a growth mindset: Embrace challenges and see them as opportunities for growth. Adopting a growth mindset will help you stay positive and keep learning.
3. Continuously learn and develop new skills: Take advantage of the resources available to you, such as online courses, webinars, and professional development opportunities.
4. Stay connected with your colleagues and community: Networking is important in any career, but especially in a remote work environment where you may not have as many opportunities to connect face-to-face. Join

online communities, attend virtual events, and reach out to colleagues for support and mentorship.

5. Take care of your physical and mental health: Make sure to prioritize your health by taking breaks throughout the day, exercising regularly, and practicing stress-reducing activities like meditation or yoga.

6. Manage your time effectively: Set boundaries between work and personal time, and use time management techniques such as the Pomodoro method or time blocking to stay productive and avoid burnout.

7. Stay organized: Keep your digital and physical workspace organized and decluttered to reduce distractions and increase focus.

8. Embrace flexibility: Remote work offers a level of flexibility that traditional office environments may not, so take advantage of it to create a schedule that works best for you and your productivity.

9. Communicate effectively: Communication is key in a remote work environment, so make sure to use clear and concise language and keep your team updated on your progress.

10. Focus on delivering high-quality work: Ultimately, the most important factor in thriving in the remote workforce is consistently delivering high-quality work that exceeds expectations. Focus on producing great work and you'll naturally stand out from the crowd.

Conclusion Appendix: Resources for Remote Workers Acknowledgments

I would like to thank our readers for their interest and hope that this guide has been helpful in navigating the world of remote work.